What's Wrong, Ralph?

BY RON WEGEN

LOTHROP, LEE & SHEPARD BOOKS   NEW YORK

Sometimes

First Edition   1 2 3 4 5 6 7 8 9 10

Library of Congress Cataloging in Publication Data

Wegen, Ronald.
    What's wrong, Ralph?

    Summary: Only the reader and Ralph can see the very
strange sights that seem to surround him everywhere he
goes.   [1. Picture puzzles] I. Title.
        PZ7.W4233Wh 1984   [E]   83-19933
ISBN 0-688-02706-7   ISBN 0-688-02707-5 (lib. bdg.)

Ralph is just an ordinary boy.

But today Ralph is not seeing things in an ordinary way. Ralph's mother has just said, "Ralph, look at the clock! If you don't hurry, you and Alfred will miss the bus to the zoo."

Ralph rushed outside,
where Alfred was waiting.
"What's wrong, Ralph?"
Alfred asked.
"Oh, just 11 things,"
answered Ralph.

On the bus Ralph began to stare out the window. Alfred was puzzled.

"What's wrong, Ralph?"

"A few things," said Ralph.

At the zoo Alfred thought everything looked normal.

"Doesn't that lady look funny?" asked Ralph.

"She looks very pretty to me," replied Alfred.

"What's wrong, Ralph?"
asked Alfred.

"EVERYTHING!" laughed Ralph.

Ralph and Alfred had lunch
by the seal pool.

"Now what's wrong, Ralph?"
Alfred asked.

"Okay," giggled Ralph. "I won't."

"It's raining."

"But Ralph, there's not
a cloud in the sky."

"Now everything is noisy," said Ralph.
"It's only a barking dog," replied Alfred.

"My house looks wrong," declared Ralph.

"It looks the same as it always does," said Alfred.

"I guess I just don't have your imagination."

"I know," said Ralph. "But that's
okay. See you tomorrow."

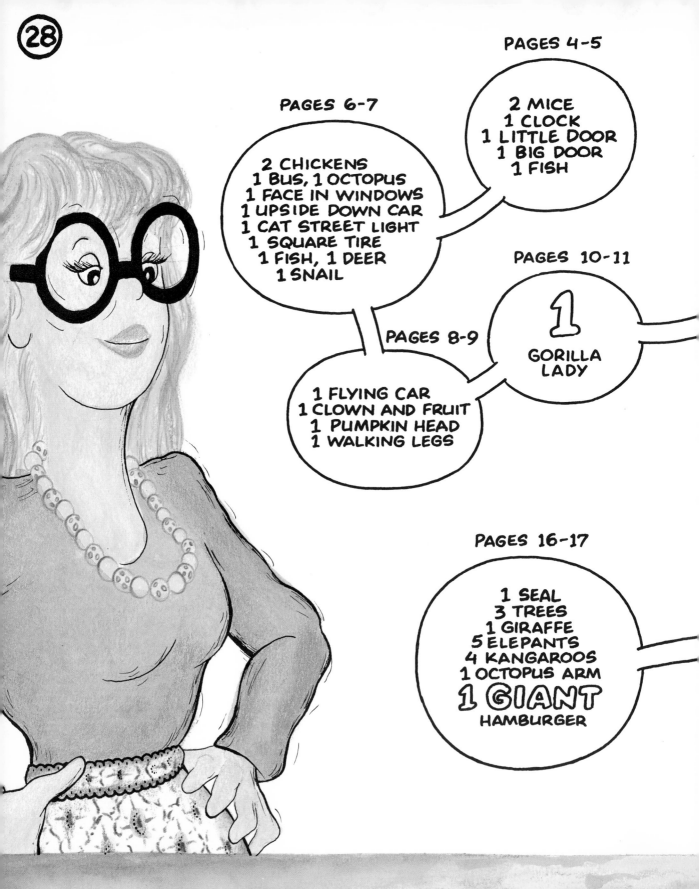

"There were lots of things

wrong today!" Ralph said.